AROUND
WOOTTON BASSETT,
CRICKLADE
AND
PURTON
IN OLD PHOTOGRAPHS

AROUND
WOOTTON BASSETT, CRICKLADE
AND
PURTON
IN OLD PHOTOGRAPHS

COLLECTED BY
TONY SHARP

ALAN SUTTON

Alan Sutton Publishing Limited
Phoenix Mill · Far Thrupp · Stroud · Gloucestershire

First Published 1990

British Library Cataloguing in Publication Data

Sharp, Tony
Around Wootton Bassett, Cricklade and Purton in old photographs.
1. Wiltshire. Wootton Bassett, history
I. Title
942.312

ISBN 0–86299–832–8

Front Cover Illustration:
PRIMITIVE METHODIST SUNDAY SCHOOL RALLY in the Wootton Bassett High Street, in the 1890s.

Typeset in 9/10 Korinna.
Typesetting and origination by
Alan Sutton Publishing Limited.
Printed in Great Britain by
Dotesios Printers Limited.

CONTENTS

INTRODUCTION 7

1. WOOTTON BASSETT 11

2. CRICKLADE 91

3. PURTON 103

4. HOOK AND THE LYDIARDS 113

5. CLYFFE PYPARD, BUSHTON, BROAD TOWN AND BROAD HINTON 119

6. LYNEHAM, TOCKENHAM AND BRADENSTOKE 129

7. BRINKWORTH 151

ACKNOWLEDGEMENTS 159

A STREET PARTY for the 1935 coronation in the High Street, outside No. 13, with the Revd and Mrs Sharp seated, and Mrs Perry and Mrs Hawkins standing behind.

VIEW OF THE TOWN HALL AND CHURCH etc. with the roadside devoid of trees, taken from Bevir's offices before 1880.

INTRODUCTION

With the interest shown in *Around Wootton Bassett in Old Photographs* and all the offers of more postcards and photographs, it was decided that a second volume would be a worthwhile project. I have tried not to duplicate material, but by the nature of things, some postcards or photographs may seem the same at first glance. For example, The Curriers' Arms outing on p. 23 in the first volume and the Curriers' outing on p. 22 of this selection may appear to be the same, but in reading the list of party members you will see a lot of fresh faces among the group.

At this point I would like to apologise to readers for the odd mistake that cropped up in the first book. In certain cases a name or a date was wrong, but at times outside information is a little bit astray, which is understandable, with memories getting somewhat hazy over the years. Sometimes the mistakes were mine, for which I have no excuse. For instance I called Miss Bartlett, Miss Guy on two occasions, which has been pointed out to me several times. Then there is the matter of the Hook Tin chapel which, in fact, still stands. I should have stated that the Hay Lane chapel, on the way to Bassett Down was the one which was pulled down. As the proverb says 'to err is Human'. I only hope those little mistakes did not detract from the pleasure of reading the book.

Another aspect of producing a book of this nature is the pleasure of receiving correspondence from people who have left the district over the years, especially the older folk, for whom the pictures have revived memories. In one instance, an elderly lady who knew Brinkworth quite well was overjoyed to be reminded of her younger days in the area.

On quite a few occasions, I have been unable to find or remember names of individual children in school groups, or adults in sporting or working parties. I would be pleased to receive any details of names etc, marked with a -?- in the captions.

Many of the places depicted in both volumes have disappeared for ever, so these trips back in time are all the more precious to the older generation who remember their towns or villages before the march of progress. For the younger folk, Wootton Bassett, Cricklade, Purton and the smaller towns and villages can be seen as they were, along with the styles of dress that we hope will never return: the broad-brimmed hats, the long, tight skirts, and lace-up boots for ladies and children; the thick worsted hard-wearing outfits and heavy hobnailed boots for men.

One childhood pleasure I was reminded of, through the photograph on p. 73, was the Sunday school outing, a real treat (no trips to the Costa Brava in those days). At first the journeys were by farm wagon to Rummings Farm, down Hook Street, to play in the fields without the fear of being chased out by an irate farmer. There were junior athletics with prizes for all who entered, and then a marvellous tea in the orchard, with big wedges of farmhouse cake all swilled down with milk straight from the cow. Then it was back to Wootton Bassett, Purton, Brinkworth, or Swindon, depending on which Sunday school one belonged to, tired and dirty, but happy.

No doubt Cricklade children had similar types of treats, but I doubt whether they would make the long journey to Rummings Farm. The Rummings family was well-known for its hospitality, and opened the farm to all the chapel Sunday schools in the area for those summer treats. Unfortunately, I have not been able to obtain a photograph of the farm. Later came the train trips to Weston-super-Mare or, for the very lucky ones, all the way to Weymouth (again, as shown on p. 73).

Another aspect of travel concerns the Hopkins' hay trussing business. Mr Hopkins was a well-known figure in the district; a familiar sight in his tweed jacket, knee breeches, knee-length woollen socks and brown shoes travelling around the countryside visiting farms, buying ricks of hay, cutting the trusses, tying and transporting it to buyers. With modern methods of haymaking, cutting and baling takes place in the fields, and the bales are put directly into barns. Mr Hopkins and his like would be hard pressed to find employment.

The old farm cottage over the top of Brynards Hill, Wootton Bassett, was completely isolated until 1938–9 (see p. 81). It was reached by a green lane from Stone-over-Lane, where Brynards Hill now is. I remember, as an errand boy for Hunts, the grocers in the High Street, struggling up that steep muddy track with a basketful of groceries on my arm. When I reached the cottage, if Miss Hacker had not shut the dog in the outhouse, I had to wait until the all-clear was given, before I could dare step inside to make my delivery. That was one of the good things of shopping in the past, a good customer could always get their goods delivered; what a difference to today's shopping. Every Saturday I had my regular deliveries to make, all winds and weathers, for the magnificent wage of 6d., $2\frac{1}{2}$p in today's values.

The houses that were built either side of Brynards Hill Lane and Stoneover Lane in 1938/9, by local builder, H. Wallis, were on offer for £500 and could be bought with a £5 deposit and a Council mortgage with fixed interest at $2\frac{1}{2}$ per cent. What a difference to today's inflated prices. The houses in Jubilee Close at Purton were also built by H. Wallis and offered at the same rates.

It is quite a problem trying to write an introduction and not cover too many of the photographs in the book with repetitive paragraphs, and if I included all the information here, there would be no captions for the photographs. All I hope is that you, the reader, will get as much enjoyment out of this book, as you did from the first volume. . .

JUBILEE PARADE in 1935. Albert Smart leading Dot the pony pulling a miniature knacker's cart, with owner Billy Strong (in slouch hat) and F. Baker the passengers.

Wootton Bassett

MISS E. PULLOM READY FOR THE OFF, at the meet of the Cricklade Hunt, outside Gittins' Shop, at the junction of High Street and Wood Street, about 1958. Among the onlookers are Mrs S. Andrews and Mrs A. Spears behind the horse, and Mrs H. Hacker below the cigarette sign.

VIEW FROM THE CHURCH TOWER looking south-west, with the old brewery building in the background. These were later used as an egg packing station by the United Dairies.

VIEW FROM CHURCH TOWER, looking south-east, towards Royal Oak. The large building, middle right, was Weston & Wallis, grocers and provisions merchants, known locally as Ragbones (see advertisement on p. 25). Later it became H. Wallis's builders offices.

HIGH STREET HILL AND ENTRANCE TO THE ROPE YARD. The piece of ground behind the Wagon & Horses, was H. Wallis's stockyard, which contained an old mortar mill, operated by a Mr Osborne. Ash was collected from the gasworks in Station Road, ground in the mill and mixed with lime to make a black mortar, used in the 1930s.

THE OLD COTTAGE between the Rope yard and the 'Wagon'. The photograph was taken about 1900.

CHURCH BELLS AFTER RECASTING. Now numbering eight instead of the original five.

A BELL-RINGERS GROUP about 1925. From left to right, back row: -?-, L. Wilson, -?-. Middle row: -?-, A. Hawkins, N. Reeves, J. Gibbs, J. Boulter, B Reeves, -?-. Front row: -?-, Miss Bartlet, -?-.

A BELL-RINGERS GROUP, 1950. From left to right, back row: J. Amor, -?-, -?-. Middle row: N. Blackman, Mr Howe, -?-, J. Reeves, E. Grierson, L. Beazley. Front row: P. Spackman, L. Wilson, Revd Sharp, E. Brooks, H. Flewelling.

WOOTTON BASSETT FOLK DANCE TEAM. From left to right, back row: -?-, J. Cook, M. Jeffries, -?-, -?-. Front row: J. Drury, J. Franklyn, K. Smith, M. Hunt, D. Boulter. Taken in 1937.

MOTHERS' UNION GROUP ON THE VICARAGE LAWN, 1952. From left to right, back row: -?-, Mrs Sproston, J. Sproston, -?-, Miss Heron, Mrs Hopkins, -?-, -?-, Mrs Harris. Second row: Mrs Page, Mrs Beazley, Mrs Reeves, Mrs Thompson, Mrs Farr, -?-, Mrs Sharp, Revd Sharp, Mrs Leighfield, Revd Barber, Mrs Boulter, Mrs Barber, -?-, Mrs Mauchan, Mrs Allen, Mrs Wheeler, Miss Giddins. Bottom row: Mrs Stickler, Miss Bartlet, Mrs Wakefield, Miss Symes, Mrs Clarke, Mrs Hawkins and Mrs Pink on the grass.

MOTHERS' UNION GROUP, about 1949, staging a missionary play. From left to right, back row: Mrs Thompson, Mrs Hobbs, Mrs Twine, -?-, Mrs Bastin, -?-, Mrs Leighfield, Mrs Boulter, Mrs Hopkins, Mrs Adams, Mrs Giles. Front row: Mrs Sharp, Mrs Alden, Mrs Goodall, Mrs Waite, Mrs Boulter.

CHURCH CHOIR, 1950. From left to right, back row: D. Boulter, Mrs D. Spackman, -?-, K. Pearce (curate), F. Eacott, T. Goddard, D. Whitaker, Revd Dicker, A. Walker, H. Solven, J. Bryant, J. Gibbs. Choirboys, back row: F.D. Barrow, R. Lewis, E. Powell, R. Gilder, T. Solven, -?-, -?-, A. Bryant. Front row: S. Loveday, -?-, David Spackman, -?-, C. Parsons.

A CHOIR OUTING TO WELLS, 1947. From left to right, back row: F. Stevens, A. Walker, R. Cook sen., R. Cook jun., D. Whitaker, Mrs Cook, C. Griffin, H. Solven, C. Hunt, Mrs White, Miss Bartlet, G. Roberts, M. Hunt. Middle row: P. Walker, D. Boulter, -?-, I. Clarke, -?-, D. Spackman. Front row: T. Solven, J. Spackman, C. White, -?-, I. Sharp, E. Powell, J. Hunt, P. Titcombe, C. Johns.

CHURCH NATIVITY PLAY, 1930.

HIGH STREET LOOKING EAST, **Beamans Lane** is just beyond the trees and railings on the right.

BEAMANS LANE, No. 1, with Mrs Loveday, Phylis and Steve, 1923. The Lane leads to Glebe Road and Vale View.

TOWN HALL. Bert Glass, a local character and his daughter Betty stand on the right-hand side.

MASLIN'S SHOP in High Street, looking east.

MASLIN'S SHOP WITH STAFF, about 1900. Note the modern gas lighting in each window with large arched globes.

MASLIN'S ADVERTISEMENT of 1916 from the church magazine.

CURRIER'S ARMS OUTING, 1936. From left to right: boy with bicycle, M. Thomas, -?-, -?-, G. Eacott, Harry 'Walrus' Hulbert (on account of his large moustache), J. Tuck, B. Bishop, T. Parker, B. Ogbourne, D. Luckwell (landlord), -?-, -?-, C. Hibbard in coach doorway, G. Clifford, C. Hunt, -?-, -?-, B. Glass, B. Brown, B. Emblin, B. Mazonawitz, E. Taylor.

T. TAYLOR at the door of No. 55 High Street, the home of his aunt, Mrs Cooksey. In later years, her son John rebuilt the house front and opened his DIY shop, then converted the premises into an office for his building firm. Now it is the Tile Shop.

LOCAL ADVERTISEMENTS from the 1916 church magazine.

A BULL-NOSED MORRIS outside Lloyds Bank. This was a popular motor car with the local farmers in the 1930s.

A ROAD HOG IN THE HIGH STREET in the 1920s.

HIGH STREET VIEW. The large building on the right housed the grocers shop of Weston & Wallis (see p. 12).

W. T. WALLIS, Grocer and Provision Merchant, 147 High St., WOOTTON BASSETT.

NOTED HOUSE FOR PROVISIONS.	SPECIAL VALUE IN TEA & COFFEE.
PRIME ENGLISH & DANISH BACON. Unequalled for flavour.	**TRY OUR 'PERFECTION' BLEND.** **2/4** per lb.
FINEST ENGLISH & COLONIAL CHEESE. Rich Ripe Gorgonzola.	Agent for 'DOCTOR'S CHINA TEA.' Will not hurt the weakest digestion. **3/-, 3/8** and **4/2** per lb.
THE FAMOUS M.V.S. BUTTER at lowest market prices.	Finest MOCHA and JAMAICA Coffee. Freshly roasted and ground.

WESTON & WALLIS ADVERTISEMENT.

SNOWCROFT COTTAGE, No. 154 High Street, a view from the garden at the rear, later known as the Little House, the home of the Bevir family.

WILLIAM & ANNIE WYATT, who lived in Snowcroft Cottage, came to Wootton Bassett in 1875. William was a signalman at Wootton Bassett station box for over thirty years (see p. 72).

A COPY OF THE CERTIFICATE PRESENTED TO SOPHIA SPACKMAN, 1 March 1862. The inscription reads 'This is to Certify Sophia Spackman has attended punctually, during the past year, that her conduct has been satisfactory and that she has made progress in the various subjects taught in the school, especially in writing and arithmetic. Signed William Bullock, Master.' The date above the lobby in the engraving reads 1858.

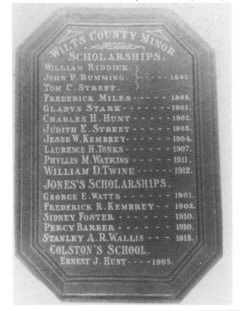

ROLL OF HONOUR from 1895 to 1905, displayed in the School Hall.

WOOTTON BASSETT COUNCIL SCHOOL, 1916. From left to right, back row: -?-, G. Blackwell, -?-, V. Twine, B. Bird, -?-, -?-, -?-, -?-. Second row: S. Hunt, G. Telling, -?-, -?-, R. Pearce. Third row: -?-, N. Nichols, N. Jeffries, V. Angel, A. Munns, G. Gough, K. Choles, W. Bull, N. Tuck. Front Row: K. Sheldon, ? Thickens, G. Thickens, H. Parsons, M. Inkpen, -?-, E. Smart. Seated: J. Tugwell.

WOOTTON BASSETT COUNCIL SCHOOL, about 1920. From left to right, back row: L. Buckland, D. Daw, -?-, -?-, N. Nash, -?-, C. Hawkins, E. Williams. Second row: ? Ody, -?-, -?-, ? Sheppard, B. Sheldon, -?-, R. Fox, D. Bull, -?-, E. Leighfield, teacher. Front row: R. Sandles, -?-, ? Edwards, -?-, -?-, -?-, -?-, A. Hawkins, G. Twine, V. Pinnock, D. Smart. Seated on mats: C. Blanchett, G. Osman, S. Simpkins, -?-.

WOOTTON BASSETT COUNCIL SCHOOL, 1920. Back row: D. Smart, T. Taylor, -?-, G. Bond, -?-, -?-, -?-. Second row: -?-, -?-, S. Hunt, -?-, -?-, M. Camden, J. Wallis, teacher. Front row: R. Sandels, W. Norris, T. Bowles, L. Brown, ? Buckland, T. Inkpen, -?-, I. Leighfield.

WOOTTON BASSETT COUNCIL SCHOOL, 1927. From left to right, back row: D. Smart, -?-, E. Williams, ? Wallis, A. Munns, G. Huxley, ? Garland, -?-, -?-. Second row: G. Bond, ? Buckland, J. Stratton, M. Inkpen, C. Clifford, C. Hawkins, G. Twine, A. Boulter, -?-, E. Leighfield. Third row: -?-, T. Ody, J. Wallis, S. Hunt, -?-, ? Harper, R. Sandels, A. Hawkins, E. Bull, G. Clifford, Mr Mew (headmaster), -?-, -?-. Fourth row: teacher, -?-, L. Brown, F. Norris, I. Leighfield, T. Bowles, P. Cooksey, G. Osman, -?-. Front row: H. Norris, D. Edwards, C. Blanchett, -?-, -?-, T. Taylor.

WOOTTON BASSETT COUNCIL SCHOOL, 1928. From left to right, back row: C. Hawkins, -?-, M. Strange, F. Munns, M. Hunt, H. Coote, -?-, L. Bowles, M. Ody. Second row: S. Hunt, J. Cook, F. Twine, -?-, T. Sheldon, F. Ody, P. Twine, ? Dixon, L. Sheppard. Third row: J. Alden, L. Wallis, D. Smart, D. Andrews, L. Inkpen, J. Newth, -?-, J. Pearce, Mr Mew. Front row: teacher, D. Price, M. Ody, M. Arthurs, B. Bull, B. Watkins, J. Perry.

WOOTTON BASSETT COUNCIL SCHOOL, 1928. From left to right, back row: N. Sheldon, P. Garland, D. Smart, M. Wallace, J. Trowbridge, D. Summers, R. Sheppard, M. Strange, B. Trowbridge. Second row: D. Thickens, M. Hunt, F. Taylor, ? Leighfield, G. Page, E. Sheppard, R. Page, Daisy Thickens, T. Taylor, ? Buckland, J. Newth. Third row: D. Bull, A. Bond, Q. Pearce, D. Price, F. Munns, M. Ody, L. Sheppard, H. Mew, P. Cooksey, L. Wallis, C. Hawkins, T. Inkpen. Front row: J. Fox, V. Stone, ? Osbourne, J. Alden, ? Bond, C. Clifford, Mr Mew (headmaster), J. Chequer, J. Cook, J. Franklyn, D. Boulter.

WOOTTON BASSETT COUNCIL SCHOOL, 1924. From left to right, back row: P. Hunt, G. Gittins, E. Rouse, J. Leighfield, E. Tuck, G. Lloyd. Second row: N. Hunt, ? Buckland, K. Flewelling, L. Ody, C. Brown. Third row: B. Crouch, K. Tuck, S. Buckland, ? Bird, F. Coote, I. Twine. Front row: Mrs Lawson (teacher), R. Alden, T. Sharp, P. Dixon, B. King, Mr Mew.

WOOTTON BASSETT COUNCIL SCHOOL, 1925. From left to right, back row: M. Ody, T. Inkpen, K. Tuck, G. Gittens, N. Hunt, P. Lloyd, N. Rouse, L. Fox, W. Hunt, ? Hunt. Second row: D. Page, ? Dixon, ? Wallis, -?-, -?-, E. Leighfield, L. Sheppard, G. Andrews, ? Ody, M. Iles, M. Harper, Miss Robins (teacher). Front row: ? Franklyn, E. Flewelling, D. Woodward, P. Henly, H. Bond, N. Trow, -?-, D. Taylor, C. Anjio.

WOOTTON BASSETT COUNCIL SCHOOL, 1928. From left to right, back row: ? King, -?-, D. Warren, ? Warren, ? Harper, ? Harper, O. Dixon, B. Smith, ? Parsons, ? Wise. Second row: L. Leighfield, -?-, V. Read, P. Smart, D. Smart, I. Radford, T. Brown, J. Read, K. Godwin, F. Taylor, J. Sharp, Miss Strange (teacher). Front row: T. Taylor, B. Twine, -?-, B. Wakefield, -?-, H. Bond, ? Taylor, -?-, R. Andrews, P. Parsons, -?-, N. Rouse.

WOOTTON BASSETT COUNCIL SCHOOL, 1932. From left to right, back row: D. Sheppard, -?-, R. Dixon, J. Sharp, V. Read, B. Coote, J. Perry. Second row: Mr Mew, ? Harper, A. Harper, D. Lawrence, ? Warren, B. Harris, B. Twine, M. Plumb, L. Mitchard, Mrs Webb (teacher). Third row: L. Inkpen, -?-, H. Collins, ? Harper, -?-, -?-, M. Dixon, D. Smart, ? Harper, ? Raven. Front row: L. Inkpen, -?-, O. Dixon, F. Taylor, H. Bond, -?-, T. Taylor, P. Moody, J. Franklyn, F. Franklyn, S. Hawkins.

WOOTTON BASSETT COUNCIL SCHOOL. Sports group with shield 1937. From left to right, back row: D. Sheppard, J. Perry, E. Watts, B. Coote, B. Bryant. Front row: S. Hawkins, K. Godwin, C. Sutton, M. Plumb.

WOOTTON BASSETT COUNCIL SCHOOL, 1937. From left to right back row: ? Ody, ? Sheppard, ? Harris, -?-, J. Franklyn, G. Hunt, B. Bennett, L. Taylor, S. Brown. Second row: H. Emblin, B. Twine, -?-, ? Everliegh, A. Ody, L. Mitchard, O. Dixon, R. Dixon, H. Collins, G. Wakefield, G. Andrews, Mr Mew. Third row: Miss Hitchings, M. Arthurs, B. Smith, J. Sharp, V. Read, G. Watts, D. Sheppard, K. Godwin, J. Perry, B. Hunt. Front row: D. Smart, P. Buckland, L. Taylor, -?-, R. Andrews, J. Wise, E. Thickens, F. Franklyn, D. Lawrence, -?-, S. Hawkins, M. Plumb, ? Inkpen.

WOOTTON BASSETT COUNCIL SCHOOL, 1933–4, From left to right, back row: -?-, M. Bird, N. Buckland, B. Stone, -?-, ? Page, P. Comley, D. Hunt, ? Bennet, ? Harper. Second row: Miss Bugg (teacher), M. Bull, -?-, -?-, A. Harper, W. Hunt, -?-, ? Harris, -?-, M. Iles, J. Wise, Mr Mew. Front row: D. Watts, B. Norris, ? Harris, B. Harris, H. Robbins, H. Taylor, H. Bond, F. Tuck, -?-, -?-, G. Wakefield.

WOOTTON BASSETT COUNCIL SCHOOL, 1934. Friday afternoon was 'Bring your own Toy time'. From left to right, back row: Miss Strange (infant teacher), G. Hillier, S. Taylor, -?-, D. Watts, -?-, -?-, -?-. Second row: -?-, -?-, B. Leighfield, -?-, D. Simpkins, D. King, -?-. Front row: B. Norris, J. Taylor, K. Hanks, B. Taylor, ? Harper, B. Harris, J. Reeves, R. Cook.

WOOTTON BASSETT COUNCIL SCHOOL netball team, 1932. From left to right, back row: B. Payne, E. Flewelling, W. Rawlins, H. Bond, E. King. Front row: E. Leighfield, Miss Hitchins (teacher), P. Garland.

WOOTTON BASSETT COUNCIL SCHOOL hockey team 1932. From left to right, back row: E. Flewelling, -?-, E. King, M. Saunders, W. Rawlins, D. Woodward, P. Garland. Front row: E. Leighfield, B. Payne, Miss Hitchings, H. Bond, P. Childs.

WOOTTON BASSETT COUNCIL SCHOOL PLAY, *Jan of Windmill Land* in the old wooden Memorial Hall in Station Road. From left to right, back row: Mr S. Paul as St Nicholas, F. Munns, B. Franklyn, C. Hawkins, P. Dixon, -?-, M. Baker, J. Alden, K. Flewelling, I. Jeffries, -?-, -?-. Second row: W. Rawlins, -?-, E. King, M. Dixon, D. King, G. Andrews, L. Ody, E. Flewelling, L. Trow. Third row: ? Lloyd, -?-, B. Barland, J. Pearce, H. Wheeler, B. Strange, -?-, -?-, -?-, -?-, P. Lloyd. Front row: N. Riddick, J. Sharp, N. Inkpen, H. Collins, B. Coote, F. Franklyn, S. Hawkins, W. Smith, O. Smart. Standing at left: ? Wallis.

A SMALL GROUP FROM THE PLAY, from left to right: -?-, K. Flewelling, B. Franklyn, C. Hawkins, H. Wheeler, G. Garland, P. Dixon, E. Baker.

CHRISTMAS FAIRIES FROM THE PLAY. From left to right, back row: -?-, O. Dixon, G. Andrews, L. Trow, E. Flewelling. Front row: D. Woodward, W. Rawlins, D. King, L. Ody, E. King, W. Smith.

WOOTTON BASSETT COUNCIL SCHOOL OUTING TO KEW GARDENS, 1934. From back to front: C. Sutton, Miss Hitchins, B. Bennet, R. Yates, ? Hanks, D. Lawrence, D. King, teacher, -?-, -?-, D. Sutton, M. Harper, I. Radford, J. Bull, M. Hunt, R. Andrews, F. Franklyn, B. Norris, P. Buckland, -?-, M. Taylor, S. Hawkins, A. Harper, D. Lawrence.

WOOTTON BASSETT SILVER TOWN BAND on parade passing the Clarendon Arms, about 1900. The Clarendon Arms was at No. 37 High Street. There was no record of the inn before 1830, so it was probably an alehouse prior to that date.

PART OF THE GEORGE VI CORONATION CELEBRATIONS in 1937, with the Red Cross contingent, and the Boy Scouts following. The boys are wearing their Baden-Powell bush hats, outside Trow's china shop.

ANOTHER TREELESS VIEW OF THE HIGH STREET with the Market House, centre right, just beyond the Cross Keys and Marks General Stores. The old house was recently demolished, and Potter's Walk Arcade was erected on the site.

HOW THE CAR PARKING USED TO BE IN THE HIGH STREET, with plenty of room for everyone. It is very different today when motorists even park on the pavements.

A QUIET STROLL IN THE HIGH STREET.

STRANGE'S GARAGE SITE, after demolition, now the wine shop and hairdressers shop. Just beyond the gap is Trow's hardware shop, No. 42 High Street, which in 1793 was an inn called The Kings Arms, which closed down in the 1830s.

J.B. TROW'S SHOP IN THE HIGH STREET. The information on the poster on the right reads 'Wesleyan Church, Wootton Bassett. The Sunday School Anniversary, on Sunday May 10th, 1923, with The Rev C.M. Ashdown B.D., with a Service of Songs, Entitled The River Singers'. The shop displays a good selection of stationery and toys.

THE SAME PREMISES CONVERTED TO A CAFÉ, run by a Mrs Stone for many years. The print shop and stores behind the shop were converted and used as the café dining space, which was always in great demand. It is now an estate agents.

STRANGE'S GARAGE with a fine selection of Ford vehicles. Trow's ironmongers is next door.

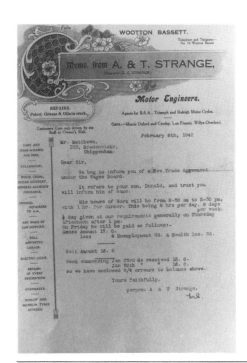

A LETTER TO MR MATHEWS OF LYNEHAM, outlining the wages payable to his son Donald. Paying the nett wage of 16s. 8d. (81½p) for a forty-eight-hour week, with a half day off, conditions permitting.

H. TROW & SONS ADVERTISEMENT. Note the price of wallpaper per roll, in old pence.

A. & T. STRANGE ADVERTISEMENT. Note the price of the bicycles. Both advertisements were taken from the church magazine 1916.

A MARKET DAY SCENE outside the Clarendon Arms.

CATTLE BEING TAKEN FROM THE MARKET PLACE by drovers, to be taken to the purchasing farmer. They are outside Barclays Bank, now the post office.

TWO VIEWS OF THE ANGEL HOTEL. Above: about 1890, with dormer windows in the roof. They sold Godwin's Ales and Stouts, from Godwins Old Town Swindon Brewery. Below: a modernized Angel, about 1930, now selling West Country Ales. Note the dormers are replaced by roof lights.

PLENTY OF ROOM TO STAND AND GOSSIP just after the turn of the century, outside Fairview the home of the Humphries family. Mr Humphries and his daughter Lucy provided plenty of entertainment for the young folk of the 1920s and '30s, with pageants and king's messengers groups, as shown in the next three photographs.

GROUP ONE. From left to right, back row: -?-, -?-, -?-, P. Beazley, -?-, E. Williams, M. Lawrence. Second row: D. Waite, -?-, M. Wallace, -?-, -?-, -?-, -?-. Third row: -?-, D. Fricker, C. Hawkins, -?-, M. Hurd, D. Hunt, J. Cook, M. Hunt, D, Hunt, -?-, -?-. Front row: J. Norris, M. Hunt, J. Merrit, N. Amor, ? Gibbs, D. Gibbs.

GROUP TWO. From left to right, back row: M. Hurd, D. Hunt, M. Wallace. Second row: -?-, J. Norris, M. Jeffries, B. Gibbs, D. Daw, R. Tucker, B. Williams, O. Farraday, J. Merrit, B. Clifford, C. Hawkins, -?-. Front row: -?-, -?-, S. Norris, P. Cooksey, J. Cook, -?-, -?-, -?-.

GROUP THREE. From left to right, back row: B. Clifford, B. Payne, O. Bailey, S. Paul, J. Cook, ? Lumley, M. Hacker. Second row: E. Williams, M. Hunt, D. Hunt, M. Griffiths, M. Hunt, E. Hawkins, M. Hurd. Front row: D. Fricker. The black faces are unrecognizable.

THE BOROUGH ARMS, about 1900. The landlady is D. Grey with L. Parkhouse on the right.

THE COTTAGE NEXT DOOR TO THE RED LION INN, No. 60 High Street at the entrance to Bug Alley, was The Lamb Inn (see p. 43 in *Around Wootton Bassett in Old Photographs*), which closed as a public house in 1907.

THE THATCHED HOUSES IN THE HIGH STREET in 1890. The last thatched house in the row was the site of Angellinettas butchers shop, later converted into the Mascot Cinema by a Mr Spears of Swindon.

THE MASCOT CINEMA with proprietor Mr Harry Hart, who bought the business from Mr Spears in the early 1920s, and carried on single-handedly as cashier and projectionist. In the days of silent films, Miss Dolly Watts of Church Street was the pianist, providing musical accompaniment to the films. On his retirement Mr Hart sold out to G. Scarrot & Son. Finally the premises reverted to a butchers shop.

HIGH JINKS IN THE HIGH STREET. Coronation Day 1937, with a fire crew from the Wootton Bassett station manning the old hand-pumped fire-engine, which worked remarkably well for its age. It is also depicted opposite.

HIGH STREET with the Angel Hotel, Smith and Hopes, Kembry's greengrocer and Sweet Shop and Apsley House (now the Apsley Arcade).

THE HIGH STREET WITH HUNT'S NEWSAGENTS SHOP on the right. Next door is Trow's Ironmongers and Strange's Garage. Trow's Shop had been The King's Arms, an inn from 1793 until it was closed down in the 1830s.

COTTAGES IN COXSTALLS, with proud mums and their up-to-date baby carriages.

CHEQUERS WORKSHOPS IN COXSTALLS, with workmen busy coffin making. The premises were later used by Mr Turner-Wright for a printing works, and later still by the Lloyd brothers as a welding and metalworks. Finally the old wooden sheds were pulled down to make a back entrance to the Roman Catholic church.

THE INKPEN CHILDREN, outside their Coxstalls cottage. Ted and Margery at the back, Tim, Noreen, Reg and Lorna in front.

WARTIME IN WOOTTON BASSETT HIGH STREET, with soldiers and children in the snow in 1940. Wootton Bassett was a staging post for the Royal Engineers early in the war. Wooden huts were erected in the Close, now Tanners Close, and on the site of the comprehensive school, with the Royal Oak and Manor House as Company Headquarters.

HENLY'S FARMHOUSE AND MANOR GARAGE. The house was demolished several years ago, along with the tin bungalows known as The Nook, when the garage forecourt was enlarged.

MRS B. BROWN OUTSIDE THE NOOK about 1920.

MR SPACKMAN, outside Tregoze House, about 1900. Tregoze House was the last house in the High Street, towards Coped Hall.

SWINDON VICTORIA FOOTBALL CLUB, a popular Swindon team who played on the Fairfield site, Coped Hall Road, above the Lime Kiln House in the 1920s and early '30s. The site is now occupied by the Mobil garage and the Lime Kiln estate.

ON THE CORNER OF STATION ROAD, No. 142 High Street, the home of the Maundrel family for many years. The last occupant was J. Bart, a member of Bevirs, the Wootton Bassett solicitors. The cottage was pulled down when the entrance to Station Road had to be widened to accommodate the large vehicles that are now on the roads. The property must have been the only remaining Elizabethan building in the town except for Priory Cottage in Wood Street.

THE START OF THE DEMOLITION OF THE ROYAL OAK, and Halls warehouse, seen from Station Road, in 1961.

WOOTTON BASSETT BOWLS TEAM. Winners of the 1955 bowls championships.

WOOTTON BASSETT BOWLS TEAM CLUB MEMBERS, 1930s. From left to right, back row: F. Twine, F. Stratton, -?-, P. Mew, W. Alden, -?-, -?-, V. Wiltshire, -?-, ? Neal, -?-. Middle row: Mrs Blackwell, -?-, -?-, Revd Barber, Mrs Barber, D. Boulter, B. Boulter. Front row: J. Trow, F. Blackwell, F. Stevens, H. Weston, P. Moody, E. Riddick, -?-.

THE ROSE QUEEN PAGEANT, held annually on the extensive lawns at the back of the Old Vicarage in Station Road, in the late 1930s. It was run in conjunction with the church fête.

THE SENIOR GIRLS' CLUB also put on displays and pageants to raise money for church funds. Back group, left to right: L. Angle, G. Telling, M. Rainger. Middle group: J. Berry, M. Taphouse, -?-, D. Boulter, P. Wells, B. Pearce, M. Franklyn, -?-, -?-. Seated: ? Skull, -?-, -?-, -?-, ? Norris, ? Reeves, B. Upton, M. Page.

AGAIN THE SENIOR GIRLS' CLUB. From left to right, -?-, B. Singer, P. Wells, M. Jeffries, M. Taphouse, D. Boulter, J. Titcombe.

SENIOR GIRLS' CLUB COUNTRY DANCE TEAM, in fours. From left to right: D. Watts, -?-, G. Hughes, ? Harris. Second group: -?-, -?-, J. Merrit, P. Saunders. Third group: S. Heath, ? Shailes, B. Hopkins, J. Titcombe.

NATIONAL SCHOOL 1947 Christmas party, held in the old YMCA Memorial Hall in Station Road.

CORONATION CARNIVAL in 1953, in the National School playground. 'Little Wife, Large Family' entry, B. Hacker, J. Pearce (in pram), M. Sharp, T. Sharp, B. Stone.

DECORATED LORRY in the 1935 Jubilee Carnival.

S. SIMPKINS AND MATE with their partially decorated lorry at the same event.

CORONATION CARNIVAL ENTRANTS, B. Clifford and Lucy Clifford ready to leave their house in Coxstall's to join the fancy dress parade in 1937.

OX ROAST IN THE CLOSE, 1937. From left to right: F. Read, B. Looms, H. Huth, P. Hunt, S. Simpkins, B. Tuck, R. Pearce, F. Northover, A. Lawrence, I. Bennett, T. Fricker, B. Simpkins, C. Haines, L. Mitchard, H. Trow and R. Spackman.

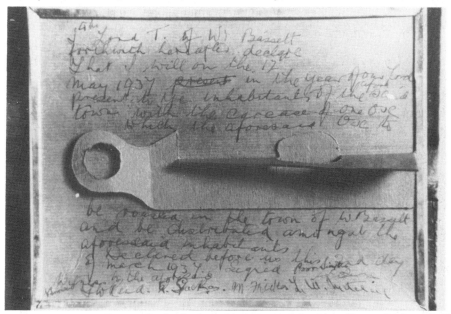

PROMISSORY NOTE, written on the back of an old photograph backing. (As read) I. Lord T Of Wt Bassett, forthwith, hereafter declare that I will, on the 12th May, 1937, in the year of our Lord, present the inhabitants of the said town, with the carcass of one Ox, which the aforesaid Ox to be roasted in the Town of W. Bassett and be distributed amongst the aforesaid inhabitants, Declared before us this 2nd Day of March 1937. Signed P — Smythe, Witnessed by the aforesaid P. Townsend, W. Read, R. Spackman, M. Fricker, L.W. Mitchard.

FANCY DRESS PARADE in the Close, 1937.

CARNIVAL PROCESSION in the High Street with B. Clifford (see p. 62) and M. Hacker with 'The Coronation Quads' in 1937.

NATIONAL SCHOOL GROUP, 1910. No names available.

NATIONAL SCHOOL GROUP, 1925. From left to right, back row: M. Curtis, M. Leighfield, J. Hunt, F. King, A. Titcombe, W. Embling, W. Reeves, W. Sheppard, M Osborne. Second row: A. Lawrence, M. Lawrence, G. Hunt, -?-, ? Drew, ? Smith, ? Smith, F. Lane, F. Eacott, R. Hopkins, Mr Searle (headmaster). Third row: M. Curtis, B. Faraday, O. Faraday, S. Faraday, -?-, H. Clark, A. Reeves, ? Smith, W. Coleman. Front row: ? Embling, J. Ruffey, F. Curtis, J. Curtis, B. Curtis, H. Reeves, ? Smith, B. Reeves, V. Hopkins, L. Clark, N. Clark, A. Embling.

NATIONAL SCHOOL GROUP, 1926, from left to right, back row: B. Gilmore, J. Amor, -?-, ? Hillier, -?-, M. Pinock, -?-, S. Grey. Second row: Mr Searle (headmaster), ? Page, D. Keen, P. Wells, D. King, -?-, -?-, -?-, Mrs Foss (teacher). Third row: -?-, -?-, B. Clifford, G. Clifford, -?-, -?-, -?-, J. Snell, -?-. Front row: -?-, A. Clifford, D. Hibbard, -?-, -?-, J. Merrit, ? Painter, M. Hind, J. Pearce, -?-, D. Snell, -?-, -?-.

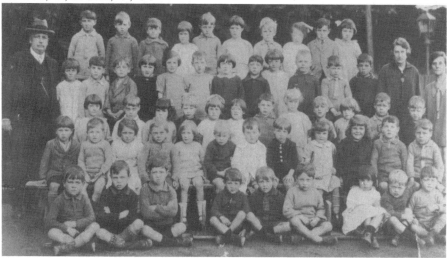

WOOTTON BASSETT NATIONAL SCHOOL, 1928. From left to right, back row: J. Pupil, -?-, -?-, F. Hibbard, R. King, K. Hacker, ? Corp, -?-, -?-, M. Parsons. Second row: Mr Searle (headmaster), -?-, -?-, -?-, A. Thompson, J. Curtis, ? Harper, -?-, -?-, -?-, J. Field, teachers Miss Gibbs and Miss Nethercot. Third row: -?-, J. Bishop, S. Norris, H. Looms, -?-, L. Clifford, J. Hacker, -?-, D. Twine, -?-, J. Reeves, ? King. Fourth row: -?-, J. Clifford, M. Lanfear, B. Hacker, S. Carter, -?-, A. Clifford, A. Harper, J. Norris, R. Norris, -?-, B. Reeves. Front row: -?-, -?-, G. Williams, R. Gibbs, S. Gibbs, ? Gibbs, ? Gibbs, L. Reeves, E. Reeves.

NATIONAL SCHOOL, 1925. From left to right, back row: -?-, E. Barber, -?-, K. Hunt, -?-, -?-, P. Hillier, D. Hunt. Second row: Mrs Cole, -?-, M. Lanfear, -?-, -?-, P. Beazley, -?-, -?-, J. Hillier, -?-, Mr Searle (headmaster). Third row: -?-, M. Hurd, B. Pupil, J. Merrit, -?-, -?-, -?-, -?-, ? Reeves, C. Hibbard, F. Hibbard. Fourth row: -?-, -?-, -?-, -?-, J. Hurd, ? Curtis, P. Hunt, -?-, -?-, -?-, -?-. Front row: C. Fry, R. Gibbs, D. Gibbs, ? Gibbs, B. Gibbs, D. Hibbard, J. Pupil, O. Lanfear, -?-, S. Amor.

NATIONAL SCHOOL, 1930. From left to right, back row: -?-, H. Hillier, M. Hind, -?-, -?-, B. Pupil, P. Wells, -?-, -?-. Second row: Mr Searle (headmaster), ? Harper, O. Lanfear, S. Amor, -?-, -?-, -?-, -?-, A. Clifford, -?-, G. Clifford, -?-, -?-, ? Harper, A. Reeves, -?-. Third row: -?-, D. Hibbard, ? Hibbard, C. Hibbard, -?-, D. Keen, -?-, B. Page, ? Beazley, Mrs Cole. Front row: B. Reeves, B. Clifford, A. Lawrence, C. Fry, -?-, O. Faraday, -?-, -?-, -?-, J. Hurd, A. Embling, -?-.

NATIONAL SCHOOL, 1954. From left to right, back row: Mr Sadler (teacher), V. Titcombe, J. Till, D. Hunt, G. Plumb, J. Reeves, M. Hutchins, J. Blackman, R. Crocker. Second row: -?-, -?-, G. Taylor, A. Evans, A. Smart, -?-, G. Cluff, T. Dash. Third row: J, Spencer, C. Merritt, D. Hibbard, V. Brown, M. Shaw, J. Gibbs. At front, V. Compton, N. Thomas.

NATIONAL SCHOOL, 1953. From left to right, back row: Mrs Parsons (teacher), P. Cottrel, A. Turk, -?-, J. Pearce, J. Karns, S. Nash, -?-, V. Cooper, D. Scarrot. Second row: -?-, -?-, B. Page, G. Hibbard, ? Parsons, -?-, -?-, B. Tyler, A. Hanks, L. Catlin, -?-, -?-. Third row: -?-, -?-, -?-, M. Freeguard, ? Brown, D. Campbell, -?-, -?-, -?-, ? Wakefield. Front row: T. Sharp, I. Campbell, J. Parker, R. Cook, D. Turnbull, S. Twine, N. Ogbourne, C. Parsons, -?-.

NATIONAL SCHOOL, 1949. From left to right, back row: Mrs Waugh (teacher), -?-, C. Merritt, D. Karns, A. Turk, ? Cottrell, J. Pearce. Second row: D. Campbell, -?-, ? Brown, -?-. Front row: S. Twine, R. Smith, -?-, N. Ogbourne, ? Gleed, ? Palmer.

NATIONAL SCHOOL, 1949. From left to right, back row: Miss James (teacher), M. Sharp, D. Pullom, J. Page, C. Hinton, P. Karns, D. Griffen, J. Selwood, S. Merritt, G. Wren, R. Amor, Miss Nethercott (teacher). Second row: S. Till, G. Hinton, C. Ody, C. Upton, P. Sterling, I. Andow, J. Ogbourne, J. Clarke, N. Crocker, K. Cottrell, I. Sharp, N. Thomas, -?-. Third row: J. Atkins, K. Scutts, G. Hancock, C. Rayner, C. Blanchett, D. Cambell, J. Ewen, E. Pullom. Front row: C. Emery, R. French, V. Hibberd, B. Purnel, G. Cuff, C. Merritt, D. Wiltshire.

NATIONAL SCHOOL, 1951/2. From left to right, back row: M. Clifford, J. Ewen, V. Cooper, ? Clark, ? Nash, A. Pilsworth, A. Turk, -?-, P. Cottrell. Second row: C. Parsons, T. Sharp, ? Gleed, ? Hanks, B. Wittaker (teacher), ? Wraite, R. Smith, G. Hibbard, G. Hanks. Third row: J. Pearce, M. Freegard, R. Hook, M. Brown. Front row: N. Ogbourne, R. Taylor, R. Cook.

WOOTTON BASSETT BROWNIES on Carnival Float, 1948.

POSTMAN WYATT of the Bungalows, Station Road, Wootton Bassett. A well-known character in the 1920s and '30s, he retired in 1933 after forty-three years in the post office. The son of signalman Wyatt of Snowcroft (See p. 26), he started work as a lad in Maslin's shop, and at the age of seventeen in 1890 was made auxiliary postman and three years later he was enrolled as a member of the permanent staff covering a variety of areas.

THE WEDDING GROUP OF MR AND MRS WILLIAMS, in the Vicarage grounds. Bride and groom, centre front; Revd and Miss Mathias are just behind the groom 1908.

A DIFFERENT VIEW OF WOOTTON BASSETT STATION (see p. 78 in *Around Wootton Bassett in Old Photographs*), with groups of passengers on both platforms. The signal box on the right has signalman Wyatt at the window (see p. 26).

A CLOSE-UP OF THE SIGNAL BOX, looking down the platform, towards Swindon.

THE PLATELAYERS' GANG, just outside the station area. 'Bant' Hunt is the second man in the front row. T. Sheldon is the other side of the foreman; other names remain uncertain.

WOOTTON BASSETT STATION. This is the 'Down' platform, with the Sunday school annual outing waiting for the Weston-super-Mare train, in 1934.

A GROUP OF HORSEMEN in Wood Street, opposite The Five Bells. The riders are F. Twine, S. Simpkins, and S. Inkpen. The onlookers are Mrs H. Beazley and son, with F. Palmer in the shop doorway.

WATTS BAKERY, in the Buthay, Church Street before renovation, after the premises were sold to the church. Charlie Watts was known as the midnight baker, making his bread during the day, and making his deliveries afternoons and evenings, often finishing his rounds between 11 and 12 o'clock at night. His customers put up with this inconvenience because his bread was the best in the district, and he was the most cheerful man you could wish to meet; he always had a laugh and a chuckle for everyone.

THE FRONT AND REAR of Nos 48 and 49 Church Street before renovation. The last tenants were old Mrs Sheldon and Harold 'Bodger' Pincott. There was a communal water tap just inside the front garden gate, behind the wall in the bottom of the top picture. This also supplied the tenants of the cottages on the other side of the road.

THE REAR OF NOS 40/41 CHURCH STREET, with G. Reeves and daughters.

MR S. HUNT OF CHURCH STREET in his new Wootton Bassett Band uniform, about 1910.

WEDDING GROUP at No. 10 Church Street. From left to right, back row: J. Wilkins, W. Price (groom), S. Hunt. Front row: F. Hunt, B. Wilkins, D. Price (bride), A. Fuller, Mrs S. Hunt, S. Hunt jun., and M. Hunt, bridesmaid.

ANOTHER CHURCH STREET BRIDE AND GROOM, Mr and Mrs H. Hacker, in their 1910 wedding finery.

THE HACKER FAMILY outside Brynards Hill Cottage: Bill, Kate, Bert and George.

THREE WELL-KNOWN WOOTTON BASSETT LADIES of the 1930s and '40s. District Nurse Bendry, Mrs Colonel Wallace, and Mrs Spackman enjoying a day at the seaside.

HAVING A WELCOME CUP OF TEA, -?-, A. Walker and B. Marshall on a Lyneham building site.

NO TEA THIS TIME for D. Andow, J. Lawrence and A. Walker on another Wallis site.

AN EARLY WOOTTON BASSETT CRICKET TEAM. Any names please?

WOOTTON BASSETT FOOTBALL TEAM, 1910.

A YOUNGER WOOTTON BASSETT FOOTBALL TEAM. Left to right, back row: S. Saunders, L. Nash, D. Cook, R. Read, P. Gillett, G. Asgough. Front row: S. Embling, G. Norris, P. Teetgen, B. Bollen, K. Pewsey, C. Simpkins.

WOOTTON BASSETT SIX-A-SIDE TEAM. Left to right, back row: L. Nash, ? Page, G. Norris. Front row: C. Merritt, P. Teetgen, C. Simpkins.

THE HOPKINS FAMILY, from left to right: Doris with Violet, Iris, Margery, Lily, Ron and Len at the back.

BARNES TIMBER TRACTOR AND LOAD by the railway near Whitehill Lane, Wootton Bassett, about 1930.

A LONG FORGOTTEN TRADE, HAY CUTTING AND TYING. Mr Hopkins is on the hayrick, with a hay knife. A. Whant is on the ladder and J. Parker attends the hay press.

MR HOPKINS cutting and his daughter Margery with a pitchfork.

THE TRUSS OF HAY IN THE PRESS being compressed ready for tying.

TRUSSES STACKED, AWAITING THE HAY WAGON, with the hay press between stack and rick.

MR HOPKINS AT RICK TOP, showing the size of the hay knife, and J. Parker lifting a freshly cut truss down to the press for tying.

CUSTOMERS OUTSIDE THE SKEW BRIDGE INN, Hunts Mill. From left to right, standing: ? Smith, H. Boulter, -?-, B. Page, O. Hyde, -?-, -?-, J. Amor. Seated: -?-, -?-, C. Fry, -?-, H. Page, Landlord Fry, -?-, -?-, -?-.

MRS I. AMOR OUTSIDE HER COTTAGE, No. 2 Hunts Mill, about 1939. Hunts Mill consisted of a row of about eleven cottages with two more attached to the millhouse on the other side of the road, at the bottom of the hill where the road bridge crosses the stream. All were demolished under a road widening scheme in the 1960s.

A GROUP OF FARMERS AT A FARM AUCTION, somewhere in the Wootton Bassett area.

THE HOME GUARD SKITTLES TEAM, 1942. From left to right, back row: 'Pebbie' Titcombe, H. Hunt, J. Stratton, H. Beasant, E. Comley, -?-, I. Hart, H. Comley, A. Walker. Front row: F. Stratton, B. Ody, C. Hatch and V. Comley.

SECTION TWO

Cricklade

A BIRD'S-EYE VIEW OF CRICKLADE.

CRICKLADE CATTLE MARKET, about 1900. As in Wootton Bassett market, cattle were more or less free to roam around. However, from 1919 cattle pens were erected in Cricklade High Street on market days.

CANAL WHARF, CRICKLADE, on the Thames and Severn Canal. The canal runs from the Golden Valley alongside the River Frome, and through the two-mile Sapperton Tunnel to Cricklade, joining the Thames at Lechlade.

THE WHITE HART HOTEL, about 1920. A canopy was erected over the main entrance door in the mid-1920s.

REAR VIEW OF THE WHITE HART.

THRESHING MACHINES ASSEMBLED IN CRICKLADE HIGH STREET, with military personnel, women's land forces, and land workers, who travelled around the area gathering hay and straw to be baled and shipped to the armed forces in France and other war zones to feed the thousands of horses and mules used by the various army units during the First World War.

HIGH STREET LOOKING NORTH. The house with the sign was the coal merchant by the name of Manning in the 1920s; later it was F. Bond.

THE PRIORY, CRICKLADE, with the war memorial on the right with cannons (see picture opposite).

CRICKLADE WAR MEMORIAL. This view was taken after the Second World War, as the old cannons were removed during the war, for armaments. The wall and seats were erected at a later date.

CARNIVAL ON 'PAUL'S CROFT' about 1928, with a group of young entrants.

ALL THE FUN OF THE FAIR. A steam roundabout with posed onlookers in about 1910.

ST SAMPSON'S CHURCHYARD AND CHURCH LANE. The right-hand cottage was the home of G. Blackwell.

THE PURTON ROAD AND DANCE COMMON.

THE BRIDGE AT HATCHETS. H. Stephens (card publisher) left the post office in 1925.

THE TOWN BRIDGE FROM THE WEST SIDE, about 1928. It was a very dry summer, which would account for the dried up river bed.

THE HIGH STREET in the early 1920s. The first shop on the left is the post office. The post-master was H. Stephens (see p. 98).

COMMON HILL, the road to Malmesbury. Colonel Fuller, Master of the Fox Hounds, lived in the house on the left.

ST SAMPSON'S CHURCHYARD AND SCHOOL.

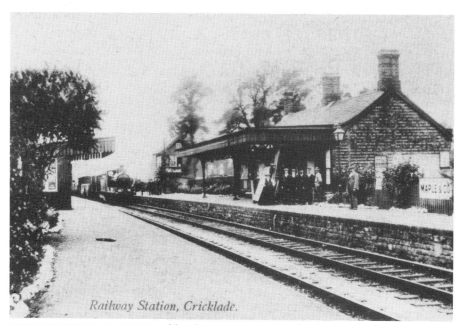

CRICKLADE STATION AND STAFF and local tradesmen waiting for the goods.

DONKEY DERBY OR PART OF CARNIVAL PROCESSION? Taken about 1900.

CRICKLADE FOOTBALL TEAM about 1900. The names are unknown.

A BAPTISM SERVICE IN THE THAMES, around the turn of the century.

SECTION THREE

Purton

PURTON WORKHOUSE. The legend on the panel over the door reads 'Cricklade and Wootton Bassett Union, 1857'. It came under the jurisdiction of the Cricklade and Wootton Bassett Rural District Council.

RED LODGE, PURTON. Once the home of Captain Ward, it is now Forestry Commission property in the Braydon Forest.

THE AVENUE LEADING TO RED LODGE. The stream under the bridge (where the white rails are) is the River Key, called the Mash Brook at the turn of the century. It runs into and out of Battle Lake.

THE OLD INSTITUTE, now the public library, at the top of Station Hill.

CHURCH PATH leading to St Mary's C. of E. School. The children posing could be pupils on their way to school.

PURTON ATHLETIC CLUB 1920/1. The third man, centre row (by the trainer's towel) is the grandson of George Bowden, shown below. Other names are uncertain.

AN OLD PURTON WORTHY, about 1880. This is George Bowden in his Sunday best.

THE ROAD TO PURTON CHURCH AND THE LYDIARDS, from Lower Square.

PURTON MANOR HOUSE, the home of Commander Walsh in the 1920s.

THE TYTHE BARN (rear view) showing the kitchen garden, part of the Manor House estate.

LOWER SQUARE, PURTON, with Webber's shop on the right and Kempster's shop by the gas lamp on the left.

THE TOLL-HOUSE, looking up Station Hill with the butchers shop and the institute at the top of the hill.

PURTON BRANCH OF THE NEW SWINDON CO-OPERATIVE STORES, opened in the 1920s.

PURTON STOKE, a quiet backwater on the Cricklade Road.

ANOTHER VIEW OF PURTON STOKE, the village of the Purton Mineral Spa.

BRAYDON SCHOOL GROUP, 1929. From left to right, back row: Mrs Evans (teacher), ? Wise, H. Matthews, ? Waldren, ? Waldren, J. Davis, J. Hussey, V Brown, D. Sheppard, Mrs O'Mara (teacher), E. Hussey, ? Vincent. Second row: M. Joyce, ? Waldren, -?-, ? Wise, J. Hussey, ? Hussey. Front row: ? Iles, R. Waldren, ? Mathews, D. Sly, R. Sly, ? Matthews.

BRAYDON SCHOOL GROUP, 1913. Names are not known.

Hook and the Lydiards

LYDIARD HOUSE, LYDIARD MILLICENT.

A LYDIARD SCHOOL GROUP, 1930. From left to right: -?-, -?-, H. Smith, -?-, M. Gleed, S. Bowler, M. Gleed. Second row: Mr Ludlow (teacher), C. Shurmer, -?-, A. Shurmer, -?-, -?-, R. Beasant, Miss Liddal (teacher). Third row: -?-, R. Rickets, T. Cottrel, J. Dixon, F. Iles. Front row: G. Bowler, R. Zala, V. Howard, S. Speed, M. Pearson, D. Cottrel.

LYDIARD SCHOOLCHILDREN WITH BLACKENED FACES IN AROUND 1930. Were they Mummers perhaps?

LYDIARD SCHOOL GIRLS' NETBALL TEAM, 1926/7. The names of these girls are not known.

LYDIARD SCHOOL FOOTBALL TEAM 1926/7. Names are uncertain.

HOOK SCHOOL, about 1930. Headmaster was Mr Leighton, teachers were Mesdames Coleman and Whittle.

THE EDMONDS FAMILY in 1904 outside 'Hat Chat' Cottage, Hook, just past the Bolingbroke Arms, towards Greatfield. They later moved to Coped Hall Agriculture Depot.

A GROUP OF GREENHILL BOYS PLAYING SOLDIERS in 1930. From left to right: R Beasant, F. Beasant, L. Titcombe, B. Beasant, R. Titcombe; S. Saunders is in the front.

A GREENHILL FAMILY in the 1920s. Three generations of the Bull family: father, daughter and granddaughter.

ANOTHER VIEW OF BASSETT DOWN HOUSE, with staff posing on the stone stairway (see p. 125 in *Around Wootton Bassett in Old Photographs*).

SECTION FIVE

Clyffe Pypard, Bushton, Broad Town and Broad Hinton

CLYFFE PYPARD MANOR GARDENS WITH THE LAKE.

CLYFFE HANGINGS.

LOOKING DOWN ON CLYFFE FROM THE HANGINGS.

THE LAWRENCE FAMILY, Clyffe Pypard (see p. 134 in *Around Wootton Bassett in Old Photographs*): George, Bessie, Mary, Lily, Helen, Ethel seated on her father's lap, Mr and Mrs Lawrence.

A VIEW OF THE AIRFIELD AT CLYFFE in 1940. 29 Elementary Flying Training School.

AIRCREW INSTRUCTORS AND OFFICE STAFF 29 Elementary Flying Training School.

PILOTS AND P. WELLS with de Havilland Moth trainer in the background. Pilots are Flt. Sgt. Price, F.O. Muraille, F.O. Willet and F.O. Davidson.

ADMINISTRATIVE STAFF outside staff offices.

A PLEASANT VIEW OF CLYFFE looking towards the Goddard Arms.

BROAD TOWN FARMHOUSE, about 1890, before road widening and the advent of the motor car.

BROAD TOWN before the invasion of the land speculators.

BROAD TOWN CARNIVAL, in the 1930s.

BROAD HINTON, POST OFFICE AND VILLAGE WELL.

BROAD HINTON CHURCH OF ST PETER AD VINCULA.

BROAD HINTON SCHOOL. Like other schools in the area, Broad Town and Clyffe Pypard are church schools, built in the 1880–90s.

TWO STREET VIEWS OF BROAD HINTON.

Lyneham, Tockenham and Bradenstoke

LYNEHAM VILLAGE GREEN and the White Hart Inn.

THE SCENE OF THE LYNEHAM TRAGEDY. The cottage at Barrow End between Lyneham and Bradenstoke, the home of the Franklyn brothers. One shot the other dead after a tiff.

LYNEHAM SCHOOL 1940. From left to right, back row: F. Jones, E. Coleman, J. Bunce, H. Ludlow, K. Chandler, E. Vines, M. Sly, J. Mathews. Second row: ? Martin, ? Martin, B. Jones, D. Ferris, G. Blackman, L. Martin, G. Dolman, I. Ody, P. Everleigh, N. Vines, M. Hillier, ? Russ. Third row: K. Vines, -?-, -?-, D. Sly, C. Everleigh, ? Martin, ? Martin, R. Hillier, ? Hillier. Front row: H. Ludlow, D. Ody, D. Blackman, D. Mathews, R. Telling, D. Ody.

MARY AND JOSEPH MATTHEWS AND FAMILY, at their house on Lyneham Banks.

131

MISSIONARY WEEK, 1903. Missionary week was held annually in the church field, now Church Park mobile home estate.

A COACHLOAD OF LYNEHAM FOLK, ready for a day out.

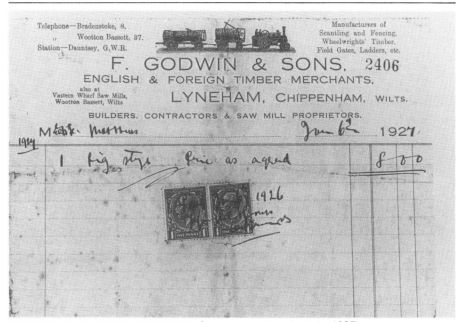

F. GODWIN & SONS, 2406

ENGLISH & FOREIGN TIMBER MERCHANTS,

also at
Vastern Wharf Saw Mills,
Wootton Bassett, Wilts.

LYNEHAM, CHIPPENHAM, WILTS.

BUILDERS, CONTRACTORS & SAW MILL PROPRIETORS.

AN INVOICE FROM GODWIN'S OF LYNEHAM, for an expensive pigsty in 1927.

A GOLDEN HANDSHAKE in 1904.

HAYMAKING AT BARROW END FARM, Lyneham 1949.

A GOOD CROP AT BARROW END. G. Kane and D. Mathews loading and G. Ferris on the tractor.

A WELL-EARNED BREAK in the hayfield for J. Goslin and M. Owens.

LYNEHAM FOOTBALL TEAM. Winners of the Chippenham Hospital Cup. From left to right, back row: -?-, L. Collins, -?-, M. Iles, D. Dunn, S. Mathews, H. Taylor, -?-, -?-, ? Mathews, -?-, -?-, -?-, -?-. Front row: D. Mathews, J. Dicks, P. Vines, with cup, -?-, D. Blackman.

LYNEHAM SCHOOL, 1911/12. From left to right, back row: M. Hunt, H. Stanley, -?-, J. Wheeler, R. Ferris, D. Thrush, F. Hillier, F. Ferris. Middle row: A. Hunt, F. Stanley, P. Hillier, D. Hillier, ? Burchel, B. Hillier, M. Wheeler. Front row: ? Wheeler, D. Jenkins, B. Ferris, ? Watson, A. Stanley, G. Hillier, ? Freeguard, ? Ovens, G. Hillier (aged three), B. Wheeler.

THE MILL HOUSE, LYNEHAM. Mr S. Nichols is sitting on the stile.

137

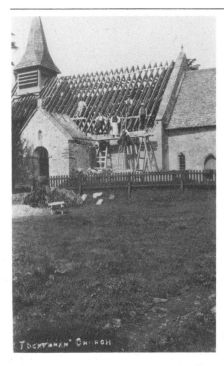

RE-ROOFING TOCKENHAM CHURCH, probably about 1920.

A TOCKENHAM FARMER ready for the shoot 1910-style.

COTTAGES AT TOCKENHAM. A little village gossip at the garden gate.

THRESHING ON A LOCAL FARM in 1917. Note the dog, Toby, waiting to catch rats.

BRADENSTOKE LADIES AND GIRLS knitting for the troops in 1916.

BRADENSTOKE CITY FOOTBALL TEAM, 1911.

BRADENSTOKE SCHOOL CHILDREN, in the late 1880s. Among this group are: I. Burchel, F. Jenkins, D. Burden, R. Edwards, G. and E. Newman.

THREE TEACHERS FROM BRADENSTOKE SCHOOL, about 1900, their names are not known.

BRADENSTOKE STREET VIEW, showing a variety of building styles, from Elizabethan to Georgian and Edwardian, and including a twentieth-century telegraph pole.

VILLAGE STREET. The girl wearing the boater-style hat is Mildred Scull. Note the half-timbered cottage.

AN EARLY ETCHING of Bradenstoke Abbey.

WORKMEN CLEANING AND NUMBERING THE ABBEY STONES as they are being pulled from the building. The man on the left is Bill Vines, the others are unknown.

THE ABBEY TOWER before dismantling.

A VIEW OF THE RUINED CRYPT.

A CLEARER VIEW OF THE STONE ARCHES in the crypt.

BRADENSTOKE PARISH CHURCH and the old Market Cross. The cottages are now demolished. The village stores are opposite.

ANOTHER VIEW OF CHURCH STREET, with Wiltshire's Stores now on the left. The house on the right is the Manor House, built about 1779–80.

KNOWN YEARS AGO AS TURKS COTTAGES, Nos 122 and 123 Bradenstoke.

A TERRACED ROW, with the chapel beyond. The cottages shown above are partly hidden by trees in the centre of the picture.

SECTION SEVEN

Brinkworth

BRINKWORTH CHURCH.

BRINKWORTH SCHOOL AND SCHOOL HOUSE, on the top of Station Hill.

Meet of the Cirencester Hounds at Brinkworth.

CIRENCESTER HOUNDS MEET on the Green before the church.

THE POST OFFICE AND GREEN. The Malmesbury Road is running from right to centre of the picture.

COTTAGES ON THE MALMESBURY ROAD.

THE THATCHED VILLAGE SHOP. The legend on the notice board over the window reads: T. Brown, General Stores.

BRINKWORTH STREET and the King's Arms.

BRINKWORTH RECTORY.

GROCERY STORES IN SOUTH VIEW. Note the old enamelled wall advertisement for Venus soap.

CHAPEL HILL, BRINKWORTH. A quiet family stroll down through the village.

CAUSEWAY END, in the pre-motor days.

TWO VIEWS OF BRINKWORTH STATION. Above with station staff and, below, looking towards Wootton Bassett, with Station Hill bridge in the background.

Anstees' Prize Turkeys. Brinkworth. 1910.

AN UNUSUAL SIGHT THESE DAYS — free-range turkeys. There were no thoughts of battery farming in 1910.

WOOD STREET, Wootton Bassett, with Stratton's Shop and Nurse Sheppard's thatched cottage and the Young Farmers' Club House, about 1956.

ACKNOWLEDGEMENTS

My thanks to the following people, for the assistance they have given to me, loaning me their postcards and old photographs, especially of the outlying areas of Cricklade, Purton, Brinkworth, Bradenstoke, etc., and for all the information to back up the illustrations.

Individual thanks to:

Mrs M. Amor • Mr B. Beasant • Miss D. Boulter • Mr A. Bowden • Mrs P. Brooks
Mrs Butler (Church Croft) • Mrs C. Duncan •Mrs M.Harrison • Mr L. Inkpen
Miss I. Jeffries • Mrs M. Mathews • Mr D. Mathews • Mr C. Ody • Mrs E. Ogbourne
Mrs L. Reeves • Mrs B. Shailes • Mr C. Simpkins • Mr P. Smart • Mr F. Stevens
Mrs A. Teetgen • Mrs L. Till • Misses M. and K. Trow • Mr J. Townsend
Mrs P. Walker • Mr P. Williams (Hinton Parva) • Mrs V. Wiltshire (Clyffe Pypard)
Miss Uzzle (Bradenstoke) • Wootton Bassett Bowls Club.

Special thanks to Mr Covey, Mr J. Davey (Cricklade) and Mr Dolbey (Brinkworth) for allowing me access to their postcard collections. I must also thank Mr Dickinson of the Swindon Museum for allowing me to purchase a copy of a photograph of the old Wootton Bassett Mascot Cinema, an unexpected bonus, as the older folk in the Wootton Bassett area will agree.

Where I have left out photographs, I apologize; unfortunately it is impossible to include every one as space is limited.